WHAT IS EXPERIENTIAL
CALVINISM?

IAN HAMILTON

REFORMATION HERITAGE BOOKS
GRAND RAPIDS, MICHIGAN

Reformation Heritage Books
2965 Leonard St. NE
Grand Rapids, MI 49525
616-977-0889 / Fax 616-285-3246
orders@heritagebooks.org
www.heritagebooks.org

Printed in the United States of America
15 16 17 18 19 20/10 9 8 7 6 5 4 3 2 1

ISBN 978-1-60178-379-0

For additional Reformed literature, request a free book list from Reformation Heritage Books at the above regular or e-mail address.

WHAT IS EXPERIENTIAL
CALVINISM?

In 1874, Charles Spurgeon wrote:

> Those who labour to smother "Calvinism" will
> find that it dies hard, and, it may be, they will
> come, after many defeats, to perceive the certain
> fact that it will outlive its opponents. Its funeral
> oration has been pronounced many times before
> now, but the performance has been premature. It
> will live when the present phase of religious mis-
> belief has gone down to eternal execration amid
> the groans of those whom it has outdone. Today
> it may be sneered at; nevertheless, it is but yes-
> terday that it numbered among its adherents the
> ablest men of the age, and tomorrow it may be,
> when once again there shall be giants in theology,
> it will come to the front, and ask in vain for its
> adversaries.[1]

Spurgeon's conviction regarding the future of Calvinism stemmed chiefly from one thing: Calvinism
was nothing less than biblical Christianity. Not

---

1. C. H. Spurgeon, *Spurgeon's Works as Published in His Monthly
Magazine "The Sword and the Trowel"* (Pasadena, Tex.: Pilgrim Publi-
cations, 1975), 4:53.

merely a humanly devised theological system, it was a system rooted in and shaped by God's revelation in Holy Scripture. It could no more die than the gospel could die, for it was the gospel in its purest form.

WHY CALVINISM IS EXPERIENTIAL

Calvinism is natively experiential. Before it is a theological system, Calvinism is deeply affectional, God-centered, cross-magnifying religion. A man may loudly trumpet his adherence to the distinctive tenets of Calvinism, but if his life is not marked by delight in God and His gospel, his professed Calvinism is a sham. In other words, there is no such thing as "dead Calvinism." Such is a theological oxymoron for one simple reason: Calvinism claims to be biblical religion, and biblical religion is not only profoundly theological, it is deeply experiential and engagingly affectional! Wherever men and women claim to be Calvinists, their lives and their ministries will pulse with life—the life of living, Spirit-inspired, Christ-glorifying, God-centered truth. This is the great feature of Calvin's *Institutes* and Owen's *Works*. They are pulsating with life!

What is experiential Calvinism? This question deserves our deepest attention. In an age when the church has been seduced by the mantra of modernity, there is a pressing need to recover the biblical gospel. There is a need to reassert with conviction and confidence those truths that gave birth to the Protestant Reformation and the Spirit-wrought transformation that is accomplished in lives invaded by such truths.

Lest you are tempted to think this is little more than an in-house Reformed debate, let me remind you that Benjamin Warfield argued that the very future of the Christian faith is inseparable from the fortunes of the Reformed faith. Where God is not the preeminent focus of the church, where man's enjoyment and not God's glory fuels the energies of the church, where programs replace prayer, where sin is reduced to a personal and societal malfunction—it is not Calvinism that dies, but the Christian faith itself.

Few of us would deny that what passes for Calvinism is often drastically removed from the passionately Trinitarian-centered, Christ-magnifying, Spirit-quickened, gospel-adoring, grace-humbling, obedience-loving religion of Calvin and his historical and theological heirs, the Puritans. For some people, Calvinism is characterized by little more than "five points," popularized in the acrostic *TULIP*. It is true that Calvinism is not less than the five points, but it is richly and profoundly more than the five points.

I well remember the first time reading John Owen. I was a young student traveling to an Inter-Varsity conference in the Scottish Borders. As I read Owen on mortification,[2] the thought gripped

---

2. John Owen, *The Works of John Owen*, ed. W. H. Goold, vol. 6, *On the Mortification of Sin* (London: Banner of Truth Trust, 1966).

me: "This man knows my heart!" That is Calvinism. Owen's exposition pulsed with life. The whole treatise breathed an atmosphere of life: pulse-quickening, heart-engaging, mind-expanding life. This is what Warfield meant when he said that the fountainhead of Calvinism does not lie in its theological system, but in its "religious consciousness." What he meant is that the roots of Calvinism are planted in a specific "religious attitude" out of which unfolds a particular theology, as day follows night. Warfield wrote, "The whole outworking of Calvinism in life is thus but the efflorescence of its fundamental religious consciousness, which finds its scientific statement in its theological system."[3]

This is what so many miss in their assessment or espousal of Calvinism. It is not first and foremost a theological system. It is more fundamentally a religious attitude, one that gives inevitable birth to a particular, precise, but gloriously God-centered and heart-engaging system of theology.

At the outset of this booklet, let me ask you a question: "Is *your* Christianity experiential and affectional?" Jonathan Edwards, the great New England pastor and theologian, began his remarkable work *Religious Affections* with a "proposition or doctrine." He said, "Who will deny that true religion consists, in a great measure, in vigorous and lively actings

---

3. Benjamin B. Warfield, *The Works of Benjamin B. Warfield* (Grand Rapids: Baker, 1981), 5:354.

of the *inclination* and *will* of the soul, or the fervent exercises of the *heart*?"[4] Edwards was deeply concerned that many professing Christians in his day (the middle decades of the eighteenth century) were contenting themselves with formal religion. It was confessionally correct, but stone cold at heart. Edwards wanted to impress on his readers "wherein true religion does consist."[5] So he wrote *A Treatise Concerning Religious Affections* to show that true Christianity is deeply and pervasively affectional. Above all, he maintained that love and joy were to be godly affections that marked true Christian profession. If your Christian profession is not marked by such affections (which may and will ebb and flow), there is a huge question mark over your profession.

The purpose of this booklet is to highlight the formative and indelible marks of experiential Calvinism. It is certainly not the aim of this booklet to suggest that Christianity is Calvinism, or that Calvinism is Christianity. However, where Christianity is rooted in the Scriptures and shaped alone by its enduring truths, what is called "Calvinism" will inevitably be found.

---

4. Jonathan Edwards, *The Works of Jonathan Edwards*, ed. Sereno Edwards Dwight and Edward Hickman (Edinburgh: Banner of Truth Trust, 1974), 1:237.

5. Edwards, *Works*, 1:235.

THE FORMATIVE PRINCIPLE OF
EXPERIENTIAL CALVINISM

What is the formative principle of Calvinism? War-field was adamant that the "formative principle" is not the doctrine of predestination, as so many imagine. Rather, it is the glory of the Lord God Almighty! This was a truth that Calvin grasped. In his treatise *On the Necessity of Reforming the Church*, a document to be presented by the leaders of the Protestant movement to the Emperor Charles V, Calvin wrote:

> If it be inquired, then, by what things chiefly the Christian religion has a standing existence amongst us, and maintains its truth, it will be found that the following two not only occupy the principal place, but comprehend under them all the other parts, and consequently the whole substance of Christianity, viz., a knowledge, first, of the mode in which God is duly worshipped; and, secondly, of the source from which salvation is to be obtained.[6]

For Calvin, the fundamental priority was not the salvation of sinners, but the right and appropriate worship of God. So the fundamental question posed in Calvinism is not how we can be saved but how God will be glorified—a question that cannot be separated from how God is to be worshiped. The Westminster Shorter Catechism in its first question

---

6. John Calvin, "On the Necessity of Reforming the Church," in *Selected Works of John Calvin: Tracts and Letters*, ed. Henry Beveridge and Jules Bonnet (Grand Rapids: Baker, 1983), 1:126.

and answer puts the matter simply but memorably: "What is the chief end of man? Man's chief end is to glorify God, and to enjoy him forever." Calvinism is compellingly and rigorously and joyfully theocentric. Romans 11:36 is the pulse beat of experiential Calvinism: "For of him, and through him, and to him, are all things: to whom be glory for ever. Amen." Let me again quote Warfield: "He who knows that it is God who has chosen him and not he who has chosen God, and that he owes his entire salvation in all its processes and in every one of its stages to this choice of God, would be an ingrate indeed if he gave not the glory of his salvation solely to the inexplicable elective love of God."[7]

It was this passionate conviction that lay behind the longing of David Brainerd for God's glory. In one of the last entries in his diary, Brainerd wrote:

> This day, I saw clearly that I should never be happy, yea, that God Himself could not make me happy, unless I could be in a capacity to "please and glorify Him forever." Take away this and admit me into all the fine havens that can be conceived of by men or angels, and I should still be miserable forever…. Oh, to love and praise God more, to please Him forever! This my soul panted after and even now pants for while I write. Oh, that God may be glorified in the whole earth.[8]

---

7. Warfield, *Works*, 5:360.

8. From the diary of Brainerd in Edwards, *Works*, 2:381.

This is the authentic spirit of experiential Calvinism. No one animated by such a spirit can be clinical or detached, far less cold and unfeeling. Samuel Rutherford, perhaps the greatest of the Scottish Puritan pastor-theologians, once wrote, "It is my greatest sorrow that I cannot get Christ lifted above the dust in Scotland." Rutherford was not unique in his pulsating passion to glorify the Savior. Occasionally I have come across people who parade their Calvinistic credentials coldly and clinically, almost as if the doctrines of grace had no more intrinsic feeling within them than the multiplication table. What they lack is the grace and tenderness of the one who does not break "a bruised reed" or quench "the smoking flax" (Isa. 42:3). No one who has been mastered by the glory of God in Christ can remain coldhearted and detached.

What, then, are we saying? Simply, *academic Calvinism* is a complete misnomer. You cannot be apprehended in any real sense by God's majestic grace and gracious majesty and not be deeply, powerfully, and permanently affected in the inner man.

Is this not a great challenge to you? Does your life and your ministry persuade people that you have been apprehended by God's majestic grace? Do others see and sense that the glory of God is the supreme passion of your life? Can they feel the tenderness of Christ as you speak to them of the unsearchable riches of the gospel?

THE FOUNDATIONAL EXPERIENCE OF EXPERIENTIAL CALVINISM

In his excellent booklet *The Practical Implications of Calvinism*, Al Martin reminds us that no passage in Scripture more confronts us with experiential Calvinism than Isaiah 6.[9] Isaiah had possibly been a prophet for some time, but here he describes for us his life-transforming encounter with the living God. In a vision he saw the Lord "high and lifted up." Isaiah was given a sight of the King, resplendent in glory, and he was never the same man again. The vision of the exalted, majestic, sovereign, holy God overwhelmed him and thereafter shaped his existence, leading him to give himself unreservedly to God's service. This is experiential Calvinism. It is the discovery that God is infinitely glorious and infinitely other than us. It is a Spirit-wrought discovery that leaves us saying with the apostle Paul: "O the depths of the riches both of the wisdom and knowledge of God! how unsearchable are his judgments, and his ways past finding out" (Rom. 11:33).

In this seminal passage, Isaiah highlights the fundamental transformative elements of his encounter with the living God. First, God's prophet was confronted with the covenant Lord's transcendent glory (vv. 1–3). The language almost defies explanation. King Uzziah had died, but *the* King lived and

---

9. Albert N. Martin, *The Practical Implications of Calvinism* (Edinburgh: Banner of Truth Trust, 1979).

reigned and ruled. Isaiah is confronted with the transitory nature of man and the everlasting kingship of Yahweh, the covenant Lord. God's prophet was being shown that God is everything.

Calvin wrote about his conversion only once in all his writings. In a passing reference in his *Commentary on the Psalms*, Calvin described himself as "subdued by God" (*Deus subegit*).[10] This is where Calvinism begins. This is the dominant note in every truly Calvinist life: "Not unto us, O LORD, not unto us, but unto thy name give glory" (Ps. 115:1).

In the Christian life, however, what truly matters is not the drama of our encounters with God in Christ, but their truth and decisiveness. While there is a prophetic uniqueness to the exalted Lord's encounter with His servant (John 12:41 tells us that it was the glory of the Son of God that Isaiah saw), every Christian is to have the identical testimony to Calvin: "I am one whom the Lord has mastered, and I now live no longer to myself but unto Him who loved me and gave Himself for me." Have you in any real measure been confronted with the Lord's transcendent glory? Is your life marked by a pervasive sense of the greatness and supremacy of God? Are you *Deus subegit*—one mastered by God?

---

10. John Calvin, *Commentary on the Book of Psalms* (Grand Rapids: Baker, 1993), 1:xl. Calvin writes, "Since I was too obstinately devoted to the superstitions of Popery to be easily extricated from so profound an abyss of mire, God by a sudden conversion subdued and brought my mind to a teachable frame [*ad docilitatem subegit*]."

Second, God's revelation of His triadic holiness, "Holy, holy, holy," brought to Isaiah a deeply felt awareness of his sinfulness (v. 3). This is the only triad in the Old Testament, and it is used to describe the Lord's profound holiness. The prophet cried out, "Woe is me! for I am undone; because I am a man of unclean lips, and I dwell in the midst of a people of unclean lips: for mine eyes have seen the King, the LORD of hosts" (v. 5). When Isaiah saw God in His kingly glory, he was not left standing. He was not left proud and dispassionate. He was deeply and irrevocably humbled. There is little doubt that Isaiah already was a believing servant. But he was a stranger to the pulse-quickened sense of God's ineffable greatness. Isaiah was beginning to see himself, perhaps for the first time, as God saw him. This is experiential Calvinism.

When you encounter God as He is, the revelation shatters all your fond imagined notions about yourself and humbles you to the dust. Isaiah was beginning to see what sin is. He was beginning to understand that the heart and horror of sin is that it is against God (Ps. 51:4). It is striking that Isaiah's conviction of sin focused on his lips: "Woe is me…for I am a man of unclean lips." He was God's prophet, the man whose lips spoke God's Word; but it was those very lips that he now confessed were "unclean." The experiential Calvinist has no fond thoughts about himself. Sin has infected and affected everything about us. But in this conviction and confession lies the beginnings of our usefulness to the Lord and His church and kingdom.

Calvinists are often accused of having "worm theology." This is actually a compliment and not an embarrassment. We are sinful worms and much worse. The devout Rutherford spoke often of his "abominable vileness," and he meant it. It is a wonder of wonders that the Lord of glory, the thrice-holy God, should love us. Yes, by the grace of Christ we are, through faith, children of the living God. But Paul could still write, "Christ Jesus came into the world to save sinners; of whom I am chief" (1 Tim. 1:15). He did not say, "I *was* the chief," but "I *am* the chief."

Is Rutherford's and Paul's sense of their abominable vileness something you can identify with? I don't mean to ask if your Christianity is morose. But I do mean this: Is your Christianity marked by sheer amazement that the Holy One should love a wretch like you? Experiential Calvinism is always marked by a deeply felt sense of sinfulness. It cannot be otherwise. This is fruitful spiritual soil. No spiritual Christlike grace can flourish in any life that has not been and is not being humbled by sin. Of all people, Calvinists have most to be humble about. If what we say about God and ourselves is truly what we believe, then *proud Calvinism* is an oxymoron!

Third, Isaiah's humbling encounter with the exalted Lord brought him a new sense of Israel's corruption (v. 5). The revelation of the majestic, exalted Lord caused Isaiah to see through the façade of

Israel's religion. He had already laid bare that façade in 1:10–20. Onlookers would have complimented Israel on the healthy state of its religion. But when a man has had a sight of the holy majesty of God, he sees not only his own sinfulness but also the sinful state of his own generation—of his own church!

It was this same conviction that led, in part, to the dismissal of Jonathan Edwards from his pastorate in Northampton. His congregation would not face up to the heart-probing nature of Edwards's biblical preaching. The outward circumstances of Edwards's dismissal might have been his concern to make the Lord's Supper a covenant meal for believers with a credible Christian profession, but the real reason was the congregation's refusal to take to heart its absence of experiential religion.

This deep-seated sense of sinfulness marks the prayers of God's people in Scripture. Daniel prayed like this to God: "*We* have sinned. *We* have not listened to your servants. *All* Israel has transgressed your law and turned aside" (see Dan. 9:5–6, 11).

Fourth, the life-shattering encounter brought Isaiah a deep, personal awareness of God's forgiving grace. As Isaiah was overwhelmed by his sinful uncleanness and undoing, God mercifully sent an angel to bring him His forgiving grace. A live coal from the altar of sacrifice, which became the symbol of the basis on which God forgives sinners, touched Isaiah's lips. Immediately God's prophet heard the words: "Lo, this hath touched thy lips; and thine iniquity is taken away, and thy sin purged" (v. 7). God's servant was being powerfully and indelibly reminded that his great need could only be met at the altar of sacrifice. He was discovering anew that the basis of his usefulness to God lay in the cleansing, renewing grace that flowed from the altar of sacrifice.

Blood atonement is an evangelical common-place. This is because it is so biblical. We talk about it, preach about it, sing about it, and write books about it. But are we continually being overwhelmed by the wonder of it? Some years ago a book was published with the title *What's So Amazing about Grace?* Calvinists know that grace is amazing. But do our lives pulse with amazement as we reflect on the Savior who loved us and gave Himself for us? Is it not the truth that we have such little sense of the sinfulness of sin and the majestic holiness of God that grace is just another word in our evangelical vocabulary? If we could see that the gulf between God and us was not a few short steps but an infinite chasm, then the cross and God's grace to us in Christ would be our glory.

To the forgiven sinner, and Calvinists who glory in God's grace to them in Christ, *forgiveness* is a humbling, overpowering, and captivating word. Nowhere is this more highlighted than in our Lord's encounter with the "sinful woman" in Luke 7:37. The extravagance of her devotion to the Lord acutely embarrassed Simon the Pharisee, Jesus' host. Jesus' response is one that ought to humble all of us: "To whom little is forgiven, the same loveth little" (v. 47). The depth of our love to the Savior is in direct proportion to the depth of our experience of and appreciation for His forgiving grace. It cannot be said too often that the primary pulse beat of the gospel is the love of God. God's love caused Him to send His only begotten Son to be the propitiation for our sins. God's love caused the apostle John to exclaim, "Behold, what manner of love the Father hath bestowed upon us, that we should be called the sons of God" (1 John 3:1). John's language is filled with unspeakable wonder. He can hardly take in the grace that is revealed in the Father's love. We could translate John's words as, "From what country is this love of the Father?" John wants us to appreciate that the Father's love is literally out of this world.

There is nothing clinical or cold in John's language; rather, it is the language of wonder. The sheer wonder of God's amazing grace—His undeserved (indeed, ill-deserved) love to judgment-deserving sinners—is not a peripheral note in Calvinism. How could it be, when God's love gave birth to the incarnation, life, death, and resurrection of our Lord Jesus Christ?

Is it not true, however, that many of us who call ourselves Reformed have lost the sense of the sheer wonder of this amazing love? Before sovereign grace is a truth to defend, it is a captivating truth to glory in.

Fifth, the dramatic encounter brought Isaiah to yield his life unreservedly to God. Isaiah's response to the Lord's question, "Whom shall I send, and who will go for us?" is immediate: "Here am I; send me" (v. 8). There was no need for the Lord to cajole or persuade Isaiah. His response to God's forgiving grace is the response of a man to whom inexplicable, sovereign grace has come.

Grace is embedded in biblical, evangelical vocabulary. But does the truth of God's grace impact our lives as it impacted Isaiah's life? God's grace costs us nothing; it is His continually undeserved, free, loving mercy. It costs us nothing, but it demands everything. Jesus made this abundantly clear to would-be followers (Matt. 8:18–22; 10:37–39). The claims of God and the service of His Son and kingdom are to have first place in our lives. Isaiah's uninhibited and unreserved response was the reflex action of a man who had seen the Lord and felt the power of His presence and grace. This is experiential Calvinism.

The story of William Borden of Yale wonderfully illustrates this point. Borden had long prepared to serve as a missionary in the Far East. He had been an outstanding student with a passion for missions. After some years traveling throughout America calling young men to go and preach the gospel of Christ, he at last set sail himself for the Far East. After reaching Alexandria in Egypt, he was struck down with cerebral encephalitis. He would never see the Far East. He would die in Alexandria. As he lay dying, he overheard someone saying, "What a waste." With the little energy he had left, Borden replied, "No reserve! No retreat! No regrets!"

This is the unreserved commitment of the experiential Calvinist. It is a life of unconditional surrender to the saving lordship of Jesus Christ. Even when the Lord searchingly tested the reality of Isaiah's unconditional allegiance (vv. 9–10), Isaiah's reaction was striking. He doesn't say, "That's not fair! Don't call me to such a work!" He simply says, "Lord, how long?" (v. 11). Isaiah is saying, "Thou art God alone. Do as Thou pleasest. All Thou doest is good and right, and I am Thine to do with as Thou pleasest." This unconditionalism is one of the pulse beats of experiential Calvinism.

What can we say then? A *proud Calvinist* is a complete misnomer. God is king, high and exalted. No man is a Calvinist because he has read Calvin or Owen, memorized the Shorter Catechism, or digested Edwards or Martyn Lloyd-Jones. A Calvinist is someone who has seen God in His majestic glory and been overwhelmed. That is why Warfield wrote, "There is nothing…against which Calvinism sets its face with more firmness than every form and degree of auto-soterism, every form of self-salvation."[11] When she was fourteen, my daughter told her teacher at her state school in a religious education lesson that she was a Calvinist. When her

---

11. Warfield, *Works*, 5:359–60.

teacher asked, "What is a Calvinist?" she replied, "Calvinists believe that God saves sinners." Experiential Calvinists bow humbly, not reluctantly, before the unimpeachable sovereignty of God and commit all they are to Him and His service.

THE FUNDAMENTAL FEATURES OF EXPERIENTIAL CALVINISM

So what then are the fundamental marks of experiential Calvinism? Calvinism is not a theological theory—a religious philosophy that compels the mind but leaves the shape of your life untouched and unmoved. Biblical truth reforms and restyles the believer's life. Calvinism leaves its indelible marks wherever it takes root in a person's life. What are those marks?

First, the experiential Calvinist honors God's unconditional sovereignty. God's sovereignty is never seen in Scripture as an excuse for believers to become passive. God's sovereignty does not suspend human responsibility but rather embraces it. But how will this manifest itself in our lives? It is shown chiefly in God's people giving themselves to consistent, faithful, heartfelt prayer. Nothing more honors God's unconditional sovereignty than prayer.

B. B. Warfield made this point forcibly: Calvinists are "humble souls, who, in the quiet of retired lives, have caught a vision of God in His glory and are cherishing in their hearts that vital flame of complete dependence on Him which is the very essence of

Calvinism."[12] It is striking and instructive to notice in the early chapters of Acts that when we encounter the church, corporate prayer is at the heart of its life: "All continued with one accord in prayer and supplication…. And they continued stedfastly in the apostles' doctrine and fellowship, and in breaking of bread, and in prayers" (Acts 1:14; 2:42; cf. 4:24–31). The demise of the church prayer meeting in recent times is deeply indicative of the spiritual atrophy that enervates the church's witness to the grace and power of the gospel. Bunyan was right when he wrote in *The Pilgrim's Progress,* "You can do more than pray after you have prayed; but you cannot do more than pray until you have prayed." Similarly, Matthew Henry wrote, "[God] requires that his people should seek unto him, and he will incline their hearts to do it, when he is coming towards them in ways of mercy…. They must pray for it, for by prayer God is sought unto, and enquired after."[13]

Can we dare call ourselves Calvinists if prayer is not one of the pulse beats of our congregational and personal life? Surely it is prayer that most manifests our conviction that God the Holy Spirit is the great convincer, convicter, and applier of Christ's saving

---

12. B. B. Warfield, *Calvin and Augustine* (Philadelphia: Presbyterian and Reformed, 1956), 496.

13. Matthew Henry, *Matthew Henry's Commentary on the Whole Bible* (Peabody, Mass.: Hendrickson, 1991), 1411.

merits to sinners. Calvinists are preeminently "pneumatic Christians."

I remember as a young student being deeply struck by a sentence in a sermon by my minister George Philip. He said, "Prayer is evangelism shorn of all its carnal attractions." He was not describing organized evangelistic endeavors. He was reminding us that evangelism that is not rooted in and saturated with prayer is a sham. Because the sovereign God alone gives the increase, we pray.

Confident dependence on God to fulfill all He has purposed is demonstrated by a life of prayer. It is only too easy in these times to take "lower ground," to resort to unbiblical expediencies in God's work. We see this in worship and evangelism where the church at times seems more influenced by principles of a fallen culture than by the precepts of God's living Word. Like Abraham, we grow weary of waiting prayerfully on God to fulfill His promises. We listen to other voices and reap a sad and sorry harvest (see Gen. 16:1–2; 17:1). Amid the struggles with the world, flesh, and devil and within a Christian evangelical culture that is drowning itself in shallowness and trivia, the experiential Calvinist draws the sweetest comfort and encouragement from knowing that the sovereign Lord is fulfilling perfectly, though mysteriously, His perfect, holy, and eternal purposes. God's sovereignty is not merely a doctrine to confess. It is a truth to rejoice in and take comfort from.

Second, the experiential Calvinist cherishes God's grace. Calvinism (though Calvin never thought that he was teaching anything other than the historic faith of the church) supremely rejoices in and placards the grace of God. Thomas Goodwin wrote eloquently about grace: "Grace is more than mercy and love, it superadds to them. It denotes not simply love, but the love of a sovereign, transcendly superior, one that may do what he will, that may wholly choose whether he will love or no.... Now God, who is an infinite Sovereign, who might have chosen whether ever He would love us or no, for Him to love us, this is grace."[14]

Experiential Calvinists are jealous to magnify the grace of God because it opens to us the heart of the God of grace: "for *Him* to love us, this is grace." When Paul comes to the end of his astonishing exposition of the gospel of God's grace in Romans 11:33–36, he can only launch into doxology:

> O the depth of the riches both of the wisdom and knowledge of God! how unsearchable are his judgments, and his ways past finding out! For who hath known the mind of the Lord? or who hath been his counsellor? Or who hath first given to him, and it shall be recompensed unto him again? For of him, and through him, and to him, are all things: to whom be glory for ever. Amen.

---

14. Thomas Goodwin, *The Works of Thomas Goodwin* (Edinburgh: J. Nichol, 1861), 2:222.

This is quintessential experiential Calvinism; indeed it is quintessential Christianity.

Third, the experiential Calvinist has a deep sense of the sinfulness of sin. It is the greatest tragedy of our age that the supreme focus in much of the Christian church today is man, not God! Man and his needs, not God and His glory, is the organizing principle and central concern of much that passes for evangelical Christianity. Perhaps the greatest difference between us and our Reformation and Puritan forefathers is that they had high views of the glory of God and therefore deep views of the sinfulness of sin. We, in contrast, have shallow, user-friendly views of God, and therefore we have shallow, user-friendly views of sin and wrath! Where do people hear today that "the *greatest evil of sin*," as Goodwin wrote, "lies in the injury by it done unto the honour and sovereign glory, and to the person of God himself, which is the thing that makes sin so heinous."[15]

We live in a world where sin has been reduced to mean little more than a personal or social inconvenience. Sin disrupts relationships, destroys families, and disfigures society—truly, it does! But Goodwin recognized that the fundamental nature of sin is its hatred of and opposition to God. Goodwin at one point dwells upon the nature and tendency of sin. He outlines three areas sin affects:

---

15. Goodwin, *Works*, 5:103.

> Now sin [1] tends to destroy God's "law," though
> it doth not; for not one iota of it shall pass; yet
> because it tends to it, as much as in it lies, Ps. cxix.
> 126, God accounts of it as destructive of his law....
> [2] So the manifestation of *God's glory*, though it
> shall receive no soil...yet sin tends to darken it
> and obscure it, and to dishonour him, setting up
> other gods.... [3] So *God's being* it toucheth not,
> yet [sin] is a "denial of God," Titus 1.16, a profess-
> ing there is none. It makes a man hate God; and
> as "he that hates his brother is a murderer," so he
> that hates God is (what in him lies) a destroyer
> of his very being; *Peccatum est Deicidium* [sin is
> God-killing].[16]

Here is someone expounding the nature of sin
biblically and theologically, not psychologically or
sociologically. This is what this present generation,
pagan and professing Christian alike, are all but
completely ignorant of: we have all but lost the sight
and sense of what sin fundamentally is. One of the
most crucial texts for the Puritans in this regard is
Psalm 51:4, "Against thee, thee only, have I sinned."
Here we are confronted both with the exceeding sinfulness of sin and its unspeakable seriousness. It is
against God! And sin sets God against us! Sin makes
us "haters of God" and God's "enemies" (Rom. 1:30;
5:8, 10). The Puritans labored to press home this truth
on the consciences of their people. Ralph Venning
wrote that sin "goes about to ungod God, and is by

---

16. Goodwin, *Works*, 5:491.

some of the ancients called *Deicidium*, God-murder or God-killing." This is not what a few "extreme" sinners seek to do: "What is done by any man would be done by every man, if God did not restrain some men from it by his power, and constrain others to obedience by his love and power."[17]

Goodwin understood well that the acme of sin's heinous nature was most manifested in the sufferings of Christ. So, he wrote, "If thou wouldst see what sin is, go to mount Calvary...as God is in himself invisible, so is the evil of sin; and as Christ is the liveliest image of the invisible God, so are his debasement and his sufferings the truest glass to behold the ugliness of sin in, and the utmost representation to make us sensible of it."[18]

George Swinnock, a contemporary of Goodwin, could have been speaking of our own day when he wrote:

> We take the size of sin too low, and short, and wrong, when we measure it by the wrong it doth to ourselves, or our families, or our neighbours, or the nation wherein we live; indeed, herein somewhat of its evil and mischief doth appear; but to take its full length and proportion, we must consider the wrong it doth to this great, this glorious, this incomparable God. Sin is incomparably

---

17. Ralph Venning, *The Sinfulness of Sin* (Edinburgh: Banner of Truth Trust, 1993), 30.

18. Goodwin, *Works*, 5:287.

> malignant, because the God principally injured by
> it is incomparably excellent.[19]

How then can people, not to mention we ourselves, be helped to see the true size and true height of sin? It is surely by seeing sin in the light of God as He is! People have such slight and superficial views of sin because they have such slight and superficial views of God! Perhaps the greatest good Goodwin could do for today's evangelical church is to reacquaint it with the sinfulness of sin.

Fourth, the experiential Calvinist lives before God's face. Experiential Calvinism has one preeminent concern: to glorify God. He recognizes that the only verdict that counts is God's. Paul told the Corinthians, "But with me it is a very small thing that I should be judged of you, or of man's judgment" (1 Cor. 4:3). He was unconcerned what verdict the church in Corinth was passing on him. He lived *coram Deo*—before God's face. It is this disposition that keeps a Christian from becoming intimidated by mere men, however impressive their credentials and spiritual pedigree. The recognition that we are what we are by the grace of God (1 Cor. 15:10) rescues us from the tyranny of man and frees us from always looking for the praise of man.

Fifth, the experiential Calvinist shapes all of life by the revelation of God's unimpeachable holiness.

---

19. George Swinnock, *The Works of George Swinnock* (Edinburgh: Banner of Truth Trust, 1992), 4:456.

God said to His people, "Be ye holy; for I am holy" (see Lev. 11:44; 1 Peter 1:16; cf. Rom. 8:29; Eph. 1:4; Titus 2:14). Every Christian has the same high and holy calling to reflect in his life the likeness of Christ, who is the image of God (Eph. 4:1–3; Phil. 2:5–8). This likeness overflows from union with Christ and is shaped and styled by God's holy commandments (John 14:15, 21). The experiential Calvinist is therefore an obedience-loving believer. God's commandments are his happy choice.

There is a profound practical implication to this "happy choice." Robert Murray M'Cheyne understood this well when he wrote, "It's not great talents that God blesses, so much as great likeness to Jesus."[20] This undeniably fundamental biblical truth must be what marks gospel preachers and theological teachers. The church needs scholarly men teaching in its seminaries; but more importantly it needs godly Christlike men teaching in its seminaries. This was one of the distinguishing hallmarks of nineteenth-century Princeton. Before Alexander, Hodge, and Warfield were noted for their intellectual abilities, they were noted for their piety. It is to be feared today that many men teaching in theological seminaries are more concerned to please the academy than they are to please God. What will impress and influence the lives of young divinity

---

20. Robert Murray M'Cheyne, *Memoir and Remains* (London: Banner of Truth Trust, 1966), 282.

students is learning soaked in gospel piety, what Calvin called *pietas*.

This piety is rooted in a love for God's law. The experiential Calvinist loves God's law. Experiential Calvinism seeks to give God's holy law the place in the believer's and church's life that God's holy Word gives it. Commenting on the phrase in Galatians 4:5, "to redeem them that were under the law," Calvin wrote: "We must here observe, the exemption from the law which Christ has procured for us does not imply that we no longer owe any obedience to the doctrine of the law, and may do whatever we please: for the law is the everlasting rule of a good and holy life!"[21] Again, commenting on Galatians 3:25, "But after that faith is come, we are no longer under a schoolmaster," Calvin wrote: "Is the law so abolished that we have nothing to do with it? I answer, the law, so far as it is a rule of life, a bridle to keep us in the fear of the Lord, a spur to correct the sluggishness of our flesh…is as much in force as ever, and remains untouched."[22] Calvin is simply echoing the teaching of Christ (John 14:15; 1 John 2:3–6).

More than ever, we need today to affirm and reaffirm the abiding relationship of God's holy law to God's holy people. This is not the prevailing view

---

21. John Calvin, *Commentaries on the Epistles of Paul to the Galatians and Ephesians* (Grand Rapids: Baker, 1993), 119.

22. John Calvin, *Galatians and Ephesians*, 109–10.

in modern evangelicalism. Thomas Manton, one of the great Puritan pastor-teachers, lived at a time when some Christians taught that God's moral law no longer applied to new covenant believers. Manton, reflecting on Jeremiah 31:31, asked believers this question: "If the law might be disannulled as to new creatures, then why doth the Spirit of God write it with such legible characters in their hearts?... Now that which the Spirit engraves upon the heart, would Christ come to deface and abolish?"[23]

John Colquhoun, in *A Treatise on the Law and the Gospel*, endorsed Calvin and Manton's understanding of the abiding relevance of God's moral law to the Christian:

> All who are united to Christ, and justified for his righteousness imputed to them, are dead to the law as a covenant; not that they may be without law to God, but that they may be under the law to Christ; not that they may continue in disobedience, but that they may be inclined and enabled to perform sincere obedience in time, and perfect obedience through eternity, to the law as a rule of life. One design of their being delivered from the obligations of the law in its Federal form is that they may be brought under the eternal obligation of it as a rule of duty in the hand of the adorable Mediator.[24]

---

23. Quoted in Ernest Kevan, *The Grace of Law: A Study in Puritan Theology* (London: Carey Kingsgate Press Limited, 1964), 157.

24. John Colquhoun, *A Treatise on the Law and the Gospel* (Grand Rapids: Soli Deo Gloria, 2009), 260.

Sixth, the experiential Calvinist is content and satisfied with scriptural worship. Submission to the unconditional sovereignty of God is seen practically in submission to the authority and sufficiency of His holy Word! This means that the experiential Calvinist seeks to have his life and the church's life contoured by "every word that proceedeth out of the mouth of the LORD" (Deut. 8:3). This means that our worship can (and must) never be shaped and informed by the fads and fashions of the moment, but by the abiding precepts and principles of God's Word. Historically, this has come to be known as the regulative principle. God has not left us to devise our own way of worship any more than He has left us to devise our own way of justification. There is such a thing as acceptable worship (Heb. 12:28). God is a "consuming fire" (v. 29), and the experiential Calvinist refuses to worship God any other way than that which He has outlined in His Word.

This in no sense means that acceptable worship will always have an antiquarian air about it. In his *Institutes*, Calvin reflects on whether "kneeling when solemn prayers are being said" is a human tradition or a divine imposition. He is clear that "the Lord in his sacred oracles...clearly expressed...all aspects of the worship of his majesty." However, Calvin goes on:

> Because he did not will in outward discipline and ceremonies to prescribe in detail what we ought to do (because he foresaw that this depended upon the state of the times, and he did not deem one

form suitable for all ages), here we take refuge
in those general rules which he has given, that
whatever the necessity of the church will require
for order and decorum should be tested against
these. Lastly, because he has taught nothing
specifically, and because these things are not nec-
essary to salvation, and for the upbuilding of the
church ought to be variously accommodated to
the customs of each nation and age, it will be fit-
ting (as the advantage of the church will require)
to change and abrogate traditional practices and
to establish new ones. Indeed, I admit that we
ought not to charge into innovation rashly, sud-
denly, for insufficient cause. But love will best
judge what may hurt or edify; and if we let love
be our guide, all will be safe.[25]

The experiential Calvinist understands that there
will of necessity be no one expression of the regulative principle of worship, but that it will be
"accommodated to the customs of each nation and
age." Calvin's concluding comment, "Let love be our
guide, [and] all will be safe," is a spiritual maxim
that is imbedded in the heart and mind of the experiential Calvinist.

Seventh, the experiential Calvinist pursues
godly catholicity. From its inception, the Reformed
faith was a multifaceted faith. To be sure it had a
well-defined core of nonnegotiable doctrines. But it
did not have and has never had one public face or

---

25. John Calvin, *Institutes of the Christian Religion* (Peabody, Mass.:
Hendrickson, 2009), 4.10.30.

particular theological expression. The Continental Reformed tradition, centered upon the Three Forms of Unity—the Heidelberg Confession, the Belgic Confession, and the Canons of Dort—is no less Reformed than its British and American Reformed counterpart within the tradition of the Westminster Standards.

This historical fact helps us to appreciate the instinctive and determined catholicity of Calvin. He was a man of strong theological convictions. He spent his life unwearyingly promoting and defending the great doctrines of the gospel recovered for the church by the grace of God. He refused to compromise, but he recognized that the Reformed faith did not have one pristine expression (though he thought his own exposition of the Reformed faith in his *Institutes* came nearest). In his letters, commentaries, treatises, and supremely in his *Institutes*, Calvin displayed a Reformed catholicity that is progressively humbling, then breathtaking, and then unsettling.

Calvin's passion for peace and unity in the church permeated all his reforming initiatives. He served the cause of Christ at a time when Protestants were visibly and bitterly divided, and from the outset he sought to heal those breaches. In a letter to Archbishop Thomas Cranmer, Calvin expressed his passionate commitment to help heal the divided body of Christ. He wrote:

> This other thing also is to be ranked among the chief evils of our time, viz., that the churches are so divided, that human fellowship is scarcely now

> in any repute among us, far less that Christian
> intercourse which all make a profession of, but few
> sincerely practice.... Thus it is that the members of
> the Church being severed, the body lies bleeding.
> So much does this concern me, that, could I be of
> any service, I would not grudge to cross even ten
> seas, if need were, on account of it.[26]

Calvin would have been mystified at how Reformed
Christians today could appear to be so indifferent
to Christ's "bleeding body." Calvin was not exhibit-
ing a personal preference in his pursuit of Reformed
catholicity. He believed, passionately, that the Word
of God commanded him to embrace everyone whom
God embraced in His Son. This was a conviction
dear to the hearts of the Westminster divines:

> Saints by profession are bound to maintain an
> holy fellowship and communion in the worship
> of God, and in performing such other spiritual
> services as tend to their mutual edification; as also
> in relieving each other in outward things, accord-
> ing to their several abilities and necessities. Which
> communion, as God offers opportunity, is to be
> extended unto all those who, in every place, call
> upon the name of the Lord Jesus.[27]

Eighth, the experiential Calvinist cultivates communion with God. The day before Owen departed
to be with Christ (August 23, 1683), he dictated his
last letter to a friend: "I am going to him whom my

---

26. Calvin, *Tracts and Letters*, 5:347–48.
27. Westminster Confession of Faith, 26.2.

soul has loved, or rather who has loved me with an everlasting love—which is the whole ground of my consolation." The following day, William Payne brought him news that his *Meditations and Discourses on the Glory of Christ* was now ready for printing. Owen replied, "I am glad to hear it; but, O brother Payne! the long wished-for day is come at last, in which I shall see that glory in another manner than I have ever done, or was capable of doing, in this world."[28] These deathbed expressions of Owen's piety confirm a truth that was, in effect, the pulse beat of Puritan piety in particular and of Calvinism in general.

Owen longed, perhaps even lived, to promote the cultivation of communion with God. He sought in his writings to encourage Christians to make communion with God a vital priority in their lives. He wrote, "Eye the Father as love; look not on him as an always lowering father, but as one most kind and tender. Let us look on him by faith, as one that hath had thoughts of kindness towards us from everlasting."[29] Christians must therefore meditate on this distinguishing, free, unchangeable love. Because he never ceased to think and feel as a pastor, Owen anticipated a query from a "trembling saint": "I cannot find my heart making returns of love unto God. Could I find my soul set upon him, I could then

---

28. Owen, *Works*, 1:111.
29. Owen, *Works*, 2:32.

believe that his soul delighted in me." To this Owen responded:

> This is the most *preposterous* course that possibly thy thoughts can pitch upon.... "Herein is love," saith the Holy Ghost, "not that we loved God, but that he loved us" first, 1 John iv. 10, 11. Now thou wouldst invert this order, and say, "herein is love, not that God loved me, but that I loved him first."... This is a course of flesh's finding out that will never bring glory to God, nor peace to thy own soul. Lay down then, *thy reasonings*; take up the love of the Father upon a *pure act of believing*, and that will open thy soul to let it out unto the Lord in the communion of love.[30]

Owen was deeply concerned that many Christians failed to grasp the grace of the Father's love in Christ:

> How few of the saints are experimentally acquainted with this privilege of holding immediate communion with the Father in love! With what anxious, doubtful thoughts do they look upon him! What fears, what questionings are there, of his good-will and kindness! At the best, many think there is no sweetness at all in him towards us, but what is purchased at the high price of the blood of Jesus.[31]

Owen never wearied of impressing on his hearers and readers that the Father's love "ought to be looked on as the fountain from whence all other

---

30. Owen, *Works*, 2:37.
31. Owen, *Works*, 2.32.

sweetnesses flow."[32] Communion with God is communion with *this* God!

Experiential Calvinism cherishes communion with God and understands that this communion requires two things: that we "receive" His love and that we "make suitable returns unto him." The Father's love is received "by faith" through Christ. "The soul being thus, by faith through Christ, and by him brought into the bosom of God, into a comfortable persuasion and spiritual perception and sense of his love, there reposes and rests itself." But there is more: "God loves, that he may be loved." So, we are to make "returns" of love to the Father.[33]

This brings us full circle. Here is what Warfield meant when he maintained that "the whole outworking of Calvinism in life is thus but the efflorescence of its fundamental religious consciousness, which finds its scientific statement in its theological system." The "fundamental religious consciousness" of experiential Calvinism is love—God's gracious love to us in Christ and the "returns" of adoring, thankful love to God in Christ.[34]

In his *Collected Works*, Goodwin considers the love of Christ, who died to make us His friends, though "he could have created new ones cheaper."[35] He continues:

---

32. Owen, *Works*, 2:22.

33. Owen, *Works*, 2:22–24.

34. Warfield, *Works*, 5:354.

35. Goodwin, *Works*, 7:193.

> Mutual communion is the soul of all true friend-
> ship…[and] friendship is most maintained and
> kept up by visits; and these, the more free and
> less occasioned by urgent business…the more
> friendly they are…. We use to check our friends
> with this upbraiding, You still come when you
> have some business, but when will you come to
> see me?… The very sight of a friend rejoiceth a
> man…. Personal communion with God is the end
> of our graces…. And as for duties, the journey's
> end of them is fellowship with God.[36]

No subject more exposes the poverty of our lives
before God than communion with God. We feel, or
we should feel, totally out of our depth. However
highly other Christians might esteem you, you know
only too well how weakly, inconstantly, poorly,
and coldly your heart engages in communion with
God. Like Paul, you desire to know Christ "and the
power of his resurrection, and the fellowship of his
sufferings" (Phil. 3:10), but how often that desire is
weakened by the sluggishness of the flesh, the diver-
sions of the devil, and the enticements of a dying
world! And yet, is not the believer's truest longing
for communion with His Savior? Even as regenerate
men and women, we are spiritual enigmas!

Thus far nothing has been said about *TULIP*,
the so-called five points of Calvinism. These five
truths—total depravity, unconditional election, limited atonement, irresistible grace, and perseverance

---

36. Goodwin, *Works*, 7:197–98.

of the saints—are biblical truths to believe and cherish. They are not the invention of Calvin. They are found in God's revealed Word, and they accent that salvation is wholly of God, that Christ's work on the cross was perfect, and that all those redeemed by Christ will be saved by Christ. But these truths can only properly (that is, *biblically*) be understood and cherished when they are set in their wider biblical context. If we extract them from their native soil, embedded as they are in the Trinitarian-centered, Christ-exalting, pastorally rich pages of Holy Scripture, they can appear and often sound metallic and clinical. Calvin understood this, and so does every truehearted experiential Calvinist.

Let me end as I began. The great question in Calvinism is, How shall God be glorified? Warfield could hardly have answered the question better:

> It is the contemplation of God and zeal for his honour which in it draws out the emotions and absorbs endeavour; and the end of human as of all other existence, of salvation as of all other attainments, is to it the glory of the Lord of all.... It begins, it centers, it ends with the vision of God in His glory: and it sets itself before all things to render to God His rights in every sphere of life.[37]

---

37. Warfield, *Works*, 5:358.